THE
SOCIAL MEDIA
PLAYBOOK
FOR
STUDENT ATHLETES

JAY IZSO
The Internet Doctor®

Published by InterAction Press
Copyright © 2018 by Jay Izso

FIRST EDITION

InterAction Press
7300 Six Fork Road
Raleigh, NC 27615
www.interaction-press.com

Cover & Interior Design:
GKS Creative, www.gkscreative.com

Library of Congress Case Number 1-6858392371

ISBN: 978-0-9915136-6-6 (paperback)
ISBN: 978-0-9915136-7-3 (e-book)

For media or booking inquiries, please contact:

STRATEGIES Public Relations
P.O. Box 178122
San Diego, CA 92177
858-467-1978
jkuritz@strategiespr.com

PRINTED IN THE UNITED STATES OF AMERICA ON ACID-FREE PAPER.

This book is dedicated to the two-part person known as the student athlete. The fact is they are students first; not only do they have to study for their academic load, but they have to be a student on the field, court, rink, or course of play. They are in constant learning mode. Their brain continues, and while other students can sit and study, their bodies now become engaged in an entirely different learning paradigm. While everyone else on campus is turning their brains off, the student athlete must keep theirs on in order to be the best they can be in their sport. Well done, fellow student athlete . . . well done!

TABLE OF CONTENTS

ACKNOWLEDGMENTS

It is really important that I thank all of the current and former student athletes whose insights, shared in conversations and interviews, guided the content of this book and showed me how I could make it more effective for them. Special thank-yous go to Ryan Boone of Presbyterian College and Abby Hansen of the University of Nebraska Omaha.

I also thank Coach Dick Portee, who says he is retired, but the truth is that he is still coaching. Maybe he's no longer coaching on the football field, but he's certainly coaching both the young and the old on the game of life. Thank you, Coach, for your great advice, your insight, your support, and, most of all, your wisdom, which have helped make this project and me successful.

I thank Jared Kuritz, my publicist and managing partner of Strategies PR, for encouraging me to write this book. Without his connecting my knowledge of social media to my love for college athletics, I am not sure this project would have ever happened.

I thank all of the college coaches I talked to, who were so honest and open with me regarding what they see as social media's role, both good and bad, in college athletics. I am truly grateful.

Finally, and most important, I give a special thank-you to my wife, Linda. She is one of the most faithful people on this planet. She believes in me and in what I do, and she always encourages me along the way.

INTRODUCTION

O K, so you are a very rare type of college student: one who is both the student and the athlete playing an organized sport for your school. Student athletes make up a very small percentage of the college and university population, yet with all of the news coverage of college sports, you would think student athletes make up the majority of the student body. You may not think about it much, but the truth is, as an athlete—right or wrong, fairly or unfairly, intentionally or unintentionally—you will be singled out by professors, other students, and people you don't even know. You are in a spotlight that doesn't catch the other students. It can be overwhelming and thrilling at the same time.

When I recall my brief college athletic career, what stands out to me is that at the time, I never realized how special it was. I also did not think about just how short the experience was going to be. One moment you are a wide-eyed, slightly hesitant, and unsure freshman, and the next thing you know you are a confident and secure senior. Then you graduate. At that point, the real world hits you, and suddenly you are that hesitant freshman again, trying to figure out your place in the universe. While this may feel like a new experience, the fact is you have been through this before, in other circumstances, whether it was when you were a freshman in high school or the first time you the rookie on your team. You must rely on those past experiences to help you navigate these different waters that you are currently swimming in.

All in all, college was a scary, crazy, fun, and amazing experience, one that I and others before and after me would never trade for anything. Believe me when I say that the relationships you form with your teammates, coaches, professors, and administrators will be part of your future. Many of them will be your friends for life. Some will help you in your career, or you may be helping them achieve their future goals. This is part of the reason why I wrote this book. You are part of an elite subgroup of people who, regardless of the level of the playing field, find yourselves in the same situation: you are all working to achieve academically in your field of study and at the same time have a gift of using your body in a very special way as an athlete, and you are attempting to perform both of those activities at the highest levels.

I've been a student, and I've been an athlete. I know what you're going through, and I'm on your side. This is why I've written this book. After my college career, I entered the field of psychology, and I went on to specialize in applying psychology to such fields as business, athletics, and the world of social media. Now, as a student-athlete alumni who has some wisdom to share, I bring you what I have watched, studied, researched, and learned to help you get the most out of social media without all the drama and the pain that many of our fellow student athletes have gone through in the past.

So, instead of calling me the Internet Doctor, think of me as your social media coach. The whistle is in my hand, but I'm not going to yell or focus only on things you are doing wrong. In this book, I am going to truly coach you on how to use social media in ways that can help you be successful not only right now but also in the future. Like your other coaches, I am going to help you get ahead by using my years of experience of walking in your shoes (or cleats!) and the wisdom I have gathered through studying the psychology and behavior of people in relation to social media; specifically, how they use social media, how they interact with others in social media, and how they use social media to influence people in positive way.

One part of college and sports that is rarely discussed is the social aspect. Perhaps some of you were like me when you first came to college: it was the first time you had complete freedom from your parents. No one was looking over your shoulder all the time. Suddenly, there were no curfews. No one was telling you to do your homework, and no one was warning you that you had to get up for school. It was your first taste of independence in many respects.

Your time is now your own, to spend and manage as you wish. The available social activities, both private and public, are numerous. Although the activities can be fun and exciting, the sheer breadth of the options can also be overwhelming. So many choices. So many people.

I think it is important for you to know that all of the student athletes before you have had to deal with plenty of the same issues that you will be wrestling with, the main dilemma being how to be a successful student and successful athlete while dealing with the social aspects of college and your new independence. None of that has changed. It is also true that if you talk to enough former student athletes, they will tell you that they did their share of things that they wish they had not done. The difference for you versus them is that when they were in school, no one had a phone that could take a picture, record a video, and instantly post either or both on the Internet so that millions of people could see them. I have had many conversations with former student athletes who have said, "I am so glad there were not smartphones when I played." This is why I firmly believe that you face a much more difficult situation as a student athlete than we did. Just when you thought you were escaping the scrutiny of the watchful eye of a parent or guardian, you have many millions of eyes potentially watching you, ready to expose you on the Internet and social media in ways you never expected. The scariest thing is that your biggest enemy on the Internet may turn out to be you, should you use social media unwisely.

I have had the privilege of working in athletics or around athletes for a large portion of my career. I played football at a National Association of Intercollegiate Athletics school. I have also worked with several sports programs at Washington State University and North Carolina State University. I love sports, but, more than that, I have great respect and love for the college student athlete. I know how hard it is to try to balance life, classes, practices, and playing time (or lack thereof) while finding time to eat, work out, hang out with friends, and be you. Regardless of what people want to think, the fact is that it's not easy being a student athlete. It's not all glory. It's not all fun. It is a ton of work. It comes with feeling good about yourself one day, when things are going well, and the next day—when things do not go quite as well—hoping that no one thinks that you don't deserve to be there. Being a student athlete is emotional. You cannot be a high-level athlete without emotions. Wins and losses matter. Playing well in your sport matters. Your college classmates who are not athletes may think they know the pressure you feel day after day, but most people do not really understand the added emotional and psychological pressure you are under in your role of athlete. I do understand it. I have lived it. I have watched it. I have counseled student athletes who were dealing with pressure from coaches, family, friends, fans, and even themselves. At times, the pressure can be so overwhelming that you may question whether being in this academic and athletic dual world is worth it. All of this is part of the price you are paying to demonstrate the athletic skills, talents, and abilities you have while being a highly productive college student.

I also understand something about your dreams and goals: how you want to prove yourself at this level and make a difference, perhaps how you dream of competing professionally. With goals like these, you end up putting a ton of pressure on yourself. I would like to tell you that this changes over time. However, the truth is, whatever you do after college—whether you play your sport at the next level or you become a professional in another industry—because of your competitive nature, you will likely always want to be the very best at what you do. You will always want to win and, moreover, you will hate to lose. This is can be a good characteristic to carry into your future. It gives you an edge over less competitive people (within reason, of course, as being competitive without self-control can have disastrous consequences). When businesses are looking for their next superstar, they are really looking for people like you, who not only want to compete but enjoy it and are willing to do what is necessary, in the right way, to be the best in their field.

In the same way that we talk about winning or losing the right way in your sport or in your future career, it is important that we talk about how social media can be a win or a loss for you as well. Like most things in life, the losses you experience while using social media will hurt you far more in your future than the victories you may achieve there will promote you. This is part of human nature and psychology. We have a tendency to focus on the one negative detail and make it so much bigger than a hundred positive things we may do. Understanding this will help you get your head around why there is so much negativity surrounding social media and athletes.

Are most athletes doing things they shouldn't on social media? No. As a matter of fact, most student athletes use social media well. However, we do not hear about those student athletes. Rather, usually we only hear about the student athletes who mess up, lose their temper, or don't think before they post on social media. It is sad, yet it is a reality of the world we live in today that you must be aware of.

I love social media. Not only is it something I use daily, but it is also something I study. Although the technology itself is interesting, my focus is on the psychology behind why people use it, how they use it, and how other people respond to what is posted. It is one of the reasons why I have written so much about it, including a previous book titled *Got Social Mediology? Using Psychology to Master Social Media for Your Business without Spending a Dime*. *Social mediology* is a term

I created that means "the study of social media from the psychology of the user, and the social psychology and culture of each platform." What I believe is most important for you when it comes to social mediology is that you observe and try to understand the psychology of the people who are using social media; observe things like who is using, what are they saying, why would they say or do that, where are they when they post (i.e., the environment) and how might that influence them, and when people use it. The more you understand the psychology of social media, the more you will be able to make good decisions about how to use it as a student athlete. The fact is that no one cares, nor will they ever really know, if you understand how Instagram or Snapchat works, but they will have an emotional reaction to every single thing that you post. This should be your most important consideration when you are debating about posting something on social media. I promise that if you think about what others' reactions might be before you post, your social media will have a far greater positive impact, and you will be able to avoid the pitfalls that other student athletes have fallen victim to.

I have several goals for this short book. My first goal is to help you avoid mistakes that have been and can be made that might cost you both today and in your future. My second goal is to give you some ideas and suggestions about social media "safe plays" so that you can use social media to your advantage both now and down the road. My third goal is to help you understand the psychology of people—that is, why we post what we post and how and why people respond the way they do to what has been posted. Ultimately, I want to give you the tools and education you need to have the easiest and smoothest path to social media success while being a student athlete and your own person, too.

I am sure that when coaches or administrators have discussed social media use with you, they have said things like, "You need to be smart when using social media," "Don't do something stupid on social media," or "You will only hurt yourself on social media." You more than likely have also received a code of conduct that addresses some of the issues associated with social media. These educational efforts may have even stirred some emotions and thoughts in you, probably along the lines of "What, are we in junior high?"

Understand that your coaches and administrators are looking at social media from a point of view that is different from yours. They bear the burden of any and all negative public relations issues for the school and team that may come up, any rules violations, and any social missteps, even when you are off campus. As a retired coach once said to me about student athletes, "We are more than just coaches: we have a responsibility to help them grow into the best women or men they can be." As coaches and administrators, they have either endured, watched, or read about the negative fallout that sometimes results from clumsy social media use. It's not surprising that their message is generally one of caution.

You may feel as though you're being treated like a child when you hear coaches and administrators admonish you about social media use. You probably think that their warnings about social media are obvious. Feeling like you're being talked down to can be very frustrating. I do understand. No one likes a lecture, especially when you probably know more about the ins and outs of the topic of discussion than the lecturer does. In this case, you likely use social media more than your coaches do, and you probably have used it longer than many of your coaches have. I can assure you that they do know that your social media use outpaces theirs, but they also have the advantages of age and life experience. It may be hard to believe, but they can anticipate hazards and roadblocks that you cannot see yet.

Your coaches are well aware that they are social media immigrants who are new to the social media world. But they are learning fast and they are smart; otherwise, they would not be coaches. They learn, they adapt, and then they apply what they know. Please give them a pass when they hand out the social media advice. I say this because, first and foremost, they are trying to protect you (and your scholarship, and your career), but they also have a responsibility to try to protect the integrity of the sports program and the university. When you get in trouble using social media, it is not only a problem for you as the athlete; it is also a problem for the coach and the school as well, because you also represent them. Therefore, everything you do, whether positive or negative, both on and off the field, reflects on them. After all, they recruited you because they thought you were a combination of a great student, a great athlete, and a great person.

That said, I would like to try an approach that's different from what you are used to. I do not want to talk about only the negatives of social media. I wish I could avoid talking about the negatives of social media entirely, but because of the few people who do bad or foolish things with it, I must address those points. However, social media has a lot that's positive going for it, too; if you use it in the right way, you will reap great benefits from it. I want to help you understand some of the psychology that can help you achieve social media fame in a way that maybe no one has talked to you about before. I am even going to introduce you to some fun psychology terms that you may not be familiar with. I will show you how what you have learned about psychology—in class, in life, and in this book—applies to this world of social media and you, the athlete.

Enjoy the read. This book is not all that long, but I hope it contributes to your success, both now and in the future! College will prove to be some of the best days of your life. It will be a mixture of ups and downs, but when you're moving your tassel to the left side of your mortarboard, I hope you will look back with no regrets. May it be all that you have hoped for and more!

Stay successful!

Jay Izso, the Internet Doctor®

1

WHAT IS SOCIAL MEDIA, REALLY?

I know you are probably saying to yourself, "I know what social media is." Well, yes, you know what the platforms are, and you certainly know how to use them. I do not need to explain Facebook to you, or how to post a picture on Instagram, or how to share a picture or video on Snapchat. What I want to talk about is this world called *social media*. What is it really? What makes it so different from anything we have seen before?

Obviously, the first part of this world is that it is social. That means that on whatever platform you are using, you more than likely have friends that you know really well, some that you know a little, and some that you really don't know, but all are following you or have friended you in some way. The purpose of social media is to either communicate or interact with these friends on various levels. It is the *social* part of social media that encourages you to interact in unique ways. You can post pictures, words, or videos that you find interesting, funny, exciting, or cool with your followers and friends. Even platforms like Snapchat, where there is very little interaction, are still a means of communication.

Many older adults and people who do not use social media struggle to understand the powerful way that social media interactions contribute to building and maintaining relationships within the social media communication system. Depending on their age and their level of technology usage, they still would rather pick up a phone, set up a meeting to look you in the eye, or send an e-mail when they want to communicate. Oh, a few will text, but even then, sometimes it doesn't feel right to them. For you and others of your generation, many relationships are created, maintained, or deepened through social media. Sometimes that is difficult for people who are not as plugged in to social media to understand, much less accept as normal.

One of the best parts of the social aspect of social media is that a post can reach many people immediately. Try doing that on a phone call! Another cool part of the social aspect is that once you post something, depending on the ease of return communication on the platform, people can and often do respond to what you've posted, triggering notifications. This is the part that excites nearly every human being who uses social media. It is gratifying and empowering to get a bunch of likes, retweets, comments, and shares as a result of something you posted. We experience positive reinforcement when we receive this kind of feedback from others for our posts, because each notification serves as additional proof that we have created something that others find likeable or worth sharing with others. When you do something on the field, court, or rink, social media is pretty much the only instrument that allows you to immediately and directly share your accomplishment with a large number of people and receive instantaneous feedback (usually congratulations for a job well done).

Look, I am no different. When someone retweets me or mentions @internetdoctor on Twitter (yes, feel free to follow me), I am checking out who it is and what he or she is saying. The social media mention means that I have either said or done something that has caused people to take notice. Some social media detractors have chalked this impulse up to low self-esteem or a need to demonstrate self-importance and status (you have probably even heard the word *narcissism* used). Sure, it could be those things, but it doesn't have to be. Reacting to feedback is simply a part of the communication process. People talk and then others respond. If we happen to say something or post a picture or video that people really like, then we get more responses. Those responses make us feel good, so we post again, fishing for more responses.

I don't want to bore you with a bunch of technical mumbo jumbo. However, you should know that research has demonstrated that we feel good about ourselves when we get feedback in our social media, but that may not be why we like social media so much. When we post something on social media, our brain releases a chemical called *dopamine* that makes us feel good, happy, even euphoric. In one study, researchers discovered that when you post, your brain actually lights up in the same areas as when you think about food, water, and, yes, sex.[1] Therefore, this whole social media thing makes us feel good: when we post, we feel good; when we receive feedback, we feel good; and then we go back for more so we can continue to feel good or even better. What I find funny about this study on posting is that when the researchers tried to pay these college students to stop posting, they refused the money. The rush of posting is just that powerful. With dopamine involved, is it any surprise that it is so difficult for those of us who use social media regularly to stop using it? However, this rush of good feelings can also be a danger for us when it comes to social media. When we are rushed with emotion, oftentimes we will do things that we would not ordinarily do when we are not feeling so emotionally flooded. When we are feeling "really good" it can, if we are not careful, lower our inhibitions and we will post things on social media we truly did not want to post. Sometimes these feelings can make you feel invincible. When this happens you may create posts or share pictures that cross a moral or ethical line as perceived by others, leading to some not-so-great consequences.

So I now turn my attention to the second word in our term of focus: *media*. Media itself is neither good nor bad. It is simply a way to publicly announce something. I can promise you that your coaches and college administrators are far more focused on this media side than they are on the social side of your social media activity. Having worked with coaches and athletes in two different Division 1 programs, I have seen firsthand that having a positive relationship with the news media is a tremendous advantage for you and your school. Having the media write good things about your coaches, team, or you is awesome, but having negative media attention, which can be created through unwise social media use, can cause many problems for you, your coaches, and your college or university. This is because when that happens, everyone involved with your school, including you, must explain why you did what you did on social media and come up with a plan to help lessen the blow to the reputations of everyone involved.

When it comes to the media aspect of social media, it is not just the news media that pays attention to what you and your team do: you must always assume that everyone is paying attention. You and I both know that because of social media, news is reported faster and with a far greater reach than ever before. What is worse is that the psychology of people is such that they pay far more attention to and remember negative activities than the positive ones. Just watch the news on television. What do you remember? It is not the few positive stories the news may air but the negative, dramatic, horrifying stories that we recall and share. To be fair, athletes say a far greater number of positive things than negative things on social media. However, if an athlete says something negative or posts an inappropriate picture or video, the media part of social media can make that tweet, post, snap (Snapchat picture or video), or gram (Instagram post) go viral in less than a minute. I know that you are really focused on the social aspect of social media. This is why you do not think of it as a big deal when you post—you're just sharing something that you think is interesting and cool or makes you look or feel good. However, the media aspect of social media pushes what you share out to the world, which can be dangerous.

Wait, I am not going negative on you. I am sympathizing with you. Odds are you got on social media long before you arrived at college. And it's hard to suddenly go from just being you with your relatively small bubble of friends to now representing your school, team, and coaches. You post thoughts, pictures, and videos while just trying to be social, then someone shares something you posted while framing it in a different way, and the next thing you know, you are being touted as the biggest monster in the world. I know, it's not fair. However, in the social digital world that we are part of, the original message that you sent can accidentally or intentionally be shared by others, often people who you do not know, and that is when you can lose control of your post.

When it comes to social media, we have to be aware of both sides of it: the fun side and the ugly side. But don't panic. As difficult as it can be, you can control your social media! As a student athlete, you may not have a ton of say in where you will go, what you will do, what time you will eat, and so on. However, you are completely in charge of your social media. Granted, different colleges and universities have different rules. For example, student athletes in certain sports make a team commitment to not use social media at all while their sport is in season. Maybe that will happen to you; regardless, you control what you do and say online.

Think of it this way: Do you say everything that comes to your mind? No, of course not. You filter your message on the basis of a lot of factors. But for some reason, many of us fail to use the same filtering process when it comes to social media. As a student of psychology, I find this fascinating. Something digital can literally last forever, whereas something we say is usually never in print and can be forgotten over time. One would think that we would be more cautious with what we write than with what we say, but it is simply not the case. So take charge of what you put on social media the same way you take charge of what you say. Control your social media message. If you can use your social media platform in a fun, positive, and social way, saying and posting the right thing at the right time, you will benefit from it. If you stay focused on the positive, your social media image and feedback will reflect that.

When the Physical Meets Social Media

Most people do not think about how their body can affect their social media use. However, I am convinced that many social media problems with not just athletes but people in general stem from the poster's body not operating efficiently. How we feel physically can most definitely affect our emotions. When we are in pain, for example, it is easy for us to snap at others because the pain lowers our ability to control our emotions. The same is true when we are tired. As a student and an athlete, you are going to have days or even weeks, such as midterms or finals week, when you push yourself to incredible physical and mental limits. When your body is under stress, such as when you are nursing an illness or injury or flirting with exhaustion, you are not in the best emotional place to use social media. Your mind is not operating at full capacity at such times, either. In such a state, it is easy to say and post things that you will regret later. My point is, pay attention to your body. You will always be best when you physically are at your best, and when you are not at your physical best, pay extra close attention to your social media posting.

THE SCOREBOARD

If you are an athlete, you are well aware that the score is important. In fact, for athletes, numbers in general are important. There are some numbers I think you should know that will give you an idea of why athletes' use of social media is such an issue.

In 2016, Fieldhouse Media interviewed more than 1,300 student athletes playing for National Association of Intercollegiate Athletes, Division 3, Division 2, and Division 1 schools.[2] What they found out about student athlete social media use may surprise you. I am not going to go through all the numbers, but I encourage you to read the survey results (see endnote 2 for the link). Some of the statistics are worth mentioning here. First of all, almost every student athlete has an account on Facebook, Instagram, Snapchat, or Twitter, and many have accounts on more than one platform. This is why the information I am sharing with you is so important: the vast majority of you are using social media. What most of you may not know is that you check your accounts more than you actually post to them. Like every other human being on the planet, you are curious. Social media is an outlet for that curiosity; we spend more time reading what others are saying than posting. And honestly, when someone overposts and clogs up our timelines, isn't that irritating? Knowing how irritating that is, most would rather comment on someone else's selfie than post one of themselves.

I have a question for you. If you were to ask every student athlete who uses social media which social media platform they most use, what do you think it would be? The answer is Twitter, but Snapchat is a close second and will more than likely surpass Twitter. As a matter of fact, recent data suggests that there are more daily users of Snapchat than there are daily users of Twitter. Here come the dangerous numbers. When student athletes were asked if they posted something inappropriate (*inappropriate* was defined as content that was racial, sexual, or violent in nature or contained profanity or references to drugs or alcohol), 45 percent of Snap-chat users admitted to doing so. That means nearly half of all student athletes have posted something they shouldn't have—something that has made them vulnerable to scrutiny and has potentially negatively affected their reputation and the reputation of their team, school, and coaches.

Do not be fooled by Snapchat. You may think it is private, you may think it goes away, but you need to know that people can take screenshots of your snaps. What is more, third-party apps can save your Snapchat videos and posts. The perception that posts are private and limited to your friends or that they disappear is a real problem. The Internet is an open source. And if you are posting on a social media platform used by hundreds of millions of people that markets itself on erasing your content, then you better believe plenty of people are going to be capturing content to ensure it never really goes away. Ask yourself a simple question: Why would you say or post something on a public forum that you would not want most people to see? The simple answer is you shouldn't. You have the power and control, so exercise it.

Here is the last number from the study, and it is the reason I am writing this book for you. When asked, 52 percent of student athletes said they have never had any social media training. Now, you may be asking, "Training? On social media?" Yes. Remember, you see social media from the social, relational, and interactional point of view. You recognize it as a quick and convenient way to get out your message to those who follow you. You are more than likely not thinking much about what you posted, how others are perceiving it, how it is interpreted, or what people may do with it, not to mention any potential negative consequences that could result when you had no intention of causing a fuss or hurt feelings. You are probably not thinking about how your post would reflect on your institution or team, because it is your account, and it is about you. I also know that many of you feel that your social media is not anyone else's business. Whether or not it should be their business, people will and do make your business their business. Unless you make all of your accounts completely private, you are really saying that others can see what you are doing and saying. You are part of a college team now, my friend, the big leagues. Many of you reading this are going to have more followers than some professional athletes do. Learning how to get the best out of social media while limiting any negative consequences is what is most important. So let's start the playbook portion of this book by looking at the positive side as well as the negative side of social media and how you can use social media in a way that gives you a better opportunity to succeed in the future.

SOCIAL MEDIA HAS CHANGED COLLEGE ATHLETICS

The sports world is always changing, especially when it comes to college athletics. Although many rule changes have affected how sports are played, equally influential is the fact that social media has removed many of the barriers between athletes and spectators. Now, nearly every action an athlete takes and every word he or she speaks or posts can be immediately afforded an unparalleled level of visibility and preserved indefinitely.

It wasn't so long ago that athletes said things that were, well, shall we say, less than socially acceptable about their political beliefs, social habits, different types of people, their own teammates and coaches, and so on. But unless the local reporter was in the room, such verbal garbage wasn't on display, documented, and distributed for public consumption. Even if it was reproduced in print, the athlete could deny the reported quotes. Now, with all of the immediacy and public attention garnered by social media, athletes no longer need to worry about a reporter: the athlete IS the reporter. Talk about cutting out the middleman! When you post, snap, tweet, and gram for all to see, you no longer need the media to come to you. As an example, on October 5, 2012, at 8:43 a.m., Cardale Jones, quarterback for the Ohio State Buckeyes, tweeted the following:

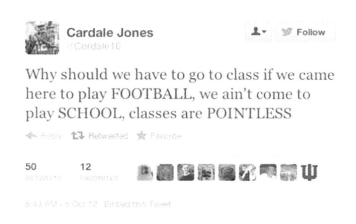

Within seconds, this tweet was retweeted, reposted, copied, and shared worldwide. Within minutes, Jones's account was closed. Too late! The tweet had already been immortalized. It will never go away. He can try to delete the tweet, close his account, or blame stupidity that the tweet even exists, but the fact of the matter is, if you type "Cardale Jones school" in Google, BAM! Right at the top of the results is where you can find a copy of his tweet.

I am sure some will say, "Well, that is just a young person doing what young people do." You may also say, "He's just sharing his opinion." And he very well may be. But that does not negate the impact that his tweet had on other student athletes, especially the overwhelming majority who will not become professional athletes and who fight every day to balance getting a good education with participating in their sport. Because Jones was a student athlete when he posted this tweet, his expressed sentiments are seen as typical of student athletes in general. Of course, you and I know this is not true, but many people see tweets like this one as reinforcing stereotypes about student athletes. His tweet also reflected, fairly or unfairly, on the coach who recruited him and ultimately on the athletic program and the university. It wasn't the media that created the firestorm; it was a student athlete using his media platform poorly who did that. He and his tweet brought the embarrassing, unwanted attention.

You could be that person; after all, you are your own media, broadcasting your message to the world. That means you have the power to do good or to do wrong. Keep in mind that right now, you are setting up your future. A slipup today may also screw up tomorrow. Just take a look at the professional athletes who have lost millions of dollars in endorsements simply by saying something they cannot take back on Twitter, Instagram, or other forms of social media. Have you ever wondered why some of the best professional athletes in their sport do not have public endorsement deals? I promise you, it is not about their acting skills. It typically is something in their social media or personal life that the company does not want to be associated with. Ryan Lochte, the Olympic swimmer, would never have lost the millions of dollars in endorsements he had locked up had he not made up a story and posted it all over social media.

But don't just look at the losses. Consider the athletes who, because they have been using social media so well, get paid every time they tweet or post about a particular product or company. In an article by The Economist, the famous soccer player Christian Ronaldo sends a Tweet out about enjoying his gift of a Tag Heuer watch. According to the article because of his high follower count across all his social media platforms, he can most likely get between $100,000 and $200,000 for one post depending on where he posts it. This is the power and money social media at its best. Let us also keep in mind, it isn't just athletes, it is anyone who has created large following counts. Look I write and speak about social media and psychology for a living. I wish someone would pay me even a quarter per tweet! I would be a tweeting machine for that product or company. Wouldn't you? If you don't want to miss out on a possible future opportunity to tweet for or be hired by a company, don't shoot yourself in the financial foot with poor social media usage now. The power to stay in the running for such a deal is (literally!) in your hands.

THE PHONE: EVERYONE IS WATCHING

Everyone has a phone. Well, I should say, everyone has a smartphone. The phones may be smart, but I sometimes wonder about the people who use them. Few people are posting to social media platforms from a laptop or desktop, some of you may use a tablet, but the phone is the primary social media tool. It is how most people check their social media profiles, take their pictures, record their video, and do their posting. In fact, some platforms like Snapchat can only be used with a smartphone. In short, your phone is how you communicate. It is perhaps the most revolutionary advancement of our time. However, in the hands of others, it is an opportunity to make themselves famous.

People want their moment of fame. If a person does not have a super talent or skill that could provide fame, what would be the fastest way for that person to get his or her fifteen minutes? At the expense of others, unfortunately. They hang around relatively famous people—oh, say, like a college athlete—hoping to catch them doing something they should not. Then they take a picture, post, and BAM! The post that they threw out in the social media sphere goes viral, and they have thousands, perhaps millions, of likes, shares, retweets, and so on. There is their fame, at the expense of others. Consider the videos that you watch on your favorite social media sites. They are not recorded on a professional camera; they are being taken by and posted from a phone, for the most part, by an amateur. Yes, there are moments when a professional photographer or media person is capturing a bad moment. However, for the most part, it is everyday ordinary people who are waiting to capture some student-athlete saying or doing something wrong, stupid, shameful, or crazy. What is more, they are waiting for someone with fame, even a small amount of fame, to fail. As a collegiate athlete, you fall into this category. If you don't want to be that person, follow the advice you have often heard from your coaches: "Keep your head on a swivel." That intentional awareness will serve you well.

Before you were born, athletes didn't have to worry about phones with cameras. They had to worry about a graduate assistant coach showing up at the party they should not be attending. Now, every person has the potential to send your coach a video of your misbehavior or, perhaps worse yet, post evidence of your drunken attempt at the Electric Slide on some social media platform. You may think you are going out in public—to a game, to a bar, to a fraternity or sorority party—to have a good time, but the problem is you may not even think about or realize you are also being photographed or filmed. You may even let yourself be filmed or photographed and not think it is a big deal. Sometimes it is not. However, chances are that one of those excursions into the real world will result in at least one picture or video that you do not want circulating for your coaches, parents, and future employers to see.

The other problem is you may be on the scene when something goes wrong. You haven't done anything, but you happen to be in the wrong place at the wrong time when something bad happens—say an argument looks to be taking a nasty turn at a party. You decide to leave, because you do not want to be a part of the drama. Too late! Someone has taken a video or a picture of you at the party. The next thing you know, you are fielding questions and accusations. You deny doing anything (because you didn't!), but because you were there and the video proves it, you are now guilty by association. Depending on the incident, a video from someone else's phone can get you called downtown to the local police department to answer some questions, even when you are completely innocent. I know, it's not fair, but that is the power of someone else's phone.

I don't think people realize that it is not necessarily the student athlete who posts reputation-shredding things on social media; other people are often happy to post evidence of the inappropriate things that athletes do. The answer to this problem is to just not put yourself in those situations. I am not saying that you can never socialize or go out with friends; I am saying it is important to use your judgment about where you go, who you hang out with, and whether you stay.

Use your phone for good causes. Take pictures with your fans. Document your visit to the local children's hospital. Share positivity. When you are walking down campus, allow people to snap a picture with you, books in hand. Heck, why not shoot a picture of lecture slide or two (provided your professor is okay with that)? Pictures and videos can be sources of endless fun and, most of the time, are not a problem, especially when you remain in control of your image. However, when you are outside of campus, even if you are eating at a restaurant with your date, just know that everyone has a phone, everyone is watching, and some people would like to steal your pride so they can become famous, even if it is for just a couple of seconds.

2

SIX MYTHS ABOUT ATHLETES AND SOCIAL MEDIA

I have found that there are six myths when it comes to athletes on social media. A myth is like a rumor: if you let other people believe it long enough, it will come to be accepted as fact.

I don't want you to fall into the trap of believing that these myths are true, so I describe and debunk them in the following text. Bust these myths and you can stay focused on playing hard, winning games, and having some fun along the way.

MYTH 1: I CAN SAY WHAT I WANT BECAUSE I AM JUST A YOUNG STUDENT

Just because you are young doesn't mean you can say and do whatever you want on social media and be forgiven. People might be kind enough to take your youth into consideration, but you can't count on it. Plus, there's a difference between forgiving and forgetting: say the wrong thing on social media and even if you are forgiven, you will have a mark on your head for the rest of your career. Take Kris Boyd, a freshman defensive back at the University of Texas. During one game, Texas was getting blown out by Texas Christian University. By halftime, the game was virtually over. Boyd went to his locker at halftime and grabbed his phone to check his social media mentions. As he looked at Twitter, he saw he was tagged in the following tweets.

Some players, fans, coaches, and administrators are probably saying, "What in the heck is this guy doing checking his phone at halftime?!" It is a great question that only Kris can answer. However, that was not Boyd's downfall. His problem was that he decided to retweet both of these to all of his followers. Some of you may be thinking, "No big deal." You would be wrong. The second tweet is from a Texas A&M fan.

"What's the problem?" you may ask. Well, Boyd is getting an athletic scholarship from the University of Texas. He signed a letter committing to the University of Texas, and the university has certain expectations regarding his conduct as a result of his signature. In one retweet—not even adding a word of his own, simply by clicking—Boyd posted a message readable by everyone in the world that makes him look like he is considering transferring. That was probably not his intent, but the damage was done. He subsequently apologized, but it didn't matter. The major media outlets ate it up. Does Boyd really want to be at the University of Texas? What does this say about University of Texas football players? Are they angry with the coach? The administrators? Are they mad about the game? Is he leaving? What the heck is going on at the University of Texas that they cannot keep their athletes from embarrassing their institution? The questions flew fast and furious.

It does not matter how young you are when you make such a misstep, because, as Boyd will soon find out, memories for mistakes are long. He is likely to find that he will always be known as the University of Texas football player who retweeted at halftime. Now there will always be extra questions about and scrutiny of everything he says or does on social media. What he thought was funny now puts him in a position where he is forever identified as the halftime retweeter. Being young comes with its benefits—unfortunately, being able to say whatever you want on social media is not one of them.

MYTH 2: PEOPLE ONLY CARE ABOUT DIVISION 1 ATHLETES' POSTS ON SOCIAL MEDIA; THEY DON'T CARE ABOUT ATHLETES' POSTS IF THEY ARE FROM DIVISION 2, DIVISION 3, OR SMALLER SCHOOLS

This is a huge myth. As an athlete, regardless of your level of play, you are under the microscope. Whether you go to a Division 1 school like Duke University, or a National Association of Intercollegiate Athletics school like Doane College, if you are an athlete, people are scrutinizing your social media use far more than the social media of the rest of the student body. You can have 10,000 athletes say and do the right thing on social media and no one cares. Yet when an athlete from a high school or small college or university says something wrong on social media, the news media uses the incident as one more example of how athletes are not really students and not all that smart; rather, they are spoiled and entitled. These stereotypes are nothing new. Portraying one person's misstep as somehow being representative of an entire group is all too commonplace.

If you say something inappropriate on social media, or perhaps even something that can be construed as reflecting poorly on your team, the consequences can end up being severe, both because you have hurt your school and because you may be made an example of. For example, in 2011, Caitlin Ortiz was on scholarship for softball at Molloy College in Long Island, New York. She posted a picture of herself with a line from a Chris Brown song: "andd imm put this drink uppp like its my lastt."

Her coach, Susan Cassidy-Lyke, immediately responded. According to Ortiz's complaint,

> *Cassidy-Lyke referred Ortiz to a printout of Ortiz's Facebook page and stated Ortiz should not have posted the typo-filled song lyric [including] "and imm put this drink upp like its my lastt"' - because she did not want recruiters to think Molloys' softball team was 'full of thugs.'*[3]

Ortiz's scholarship was taken away; Ortiz has since sued the school for discrimination. You may not think this post deserved such a serious consequence. However, coaches and administrators value and protect their team's public image. Although reposting a lyric to a popular song may seem innocent, fun, or perhaps cool, it is important for you to understand that what you do on social media can have costly consequences. Your coach and the administration are looking closely at how the members of their team reflect on the future of the team, recruiting, and public opinion. Whether you are an athlete in Division 1 or Division 3, think clearly about how everything you post affects and reflects on not only you but also the future of a program.

MYTH 3: NO ONE CARES ABOUT SPORTS OTHER THAN FOOTBALL AND BASKETBALL WHEN IT COMES TO SOCIAL MEDIA

This is false. As athletes, you are part of a very select group of people who are, fairly or unfairly, lumped under a single umbrella. It doesn't matter if you play football, volleyball, soccer, baseball, basketball, lacrosse, tennis, or underwater ping-pong (which may or may not be college sport). You are representing all athletes, both past and present, regardless of the sport you play. When one athlete says something ill-advised on Twitter, it causes people to wonder if all athletes think this way. Even if you have done nothing wrong, you occupy the category of *athlete* and take a share of the fallout. Likewise, your statements and actions on social media reflect on your fellow student athletes.

When I was working with student athletes, I remember hearing the terms *revenue sports* and *nonrevenue sports*. Of course, these terms refer to sports that make money versus those that do not make money for the athletic department.

When it comes to social media, though, it does not matter which category your sport fits into. When a student athlete makes a mistake on social media, whether or not that athlete's sport makes money for the athletic department, all of the student athletes are affected by the negativity. I am sure some of you, if not most of you, have had the experience where, when one student athlete, regardless of that athlete's sport, did something wrong on social media, every sport in the college immediately had a team meeting warning every student athlete of the dangers of social media. Student athletes who have told me about these meetings said that they tune out. They already know what is going to be said, and it sounds like a broken record of "don't do that." The flurry of meetings and warnings all stemmed from one person, in one sport, who posted something he or she should not have on social media, creating a problem for every athlete in every other sport.

MYTH 4: IF I TELL PEOPLE THAT MY ACCOUNT WAS HACKED OR SAY, "THAT WAS TAKEN OUT OF CONTEXT," PEOPLE WILL LEAVE ME ALONE

Oh, you can say this. However, the general public will not believe you, even if it is true. What is more, the news media gives a wink and nudge and makes jokes about the naiveté of the athlete who uses these types of excuses to cover up his or her social media posting sins.

I know you have seen this from college and professional athletes. An athlete will say something he or she should not have on social media, perhaps of a racial or sexual nature, or perhaps the athlete will get into an argument with a fan from another team on a social media platform. Then all of a sudden the news media catches wind of the story and it gets some airplay. The athlete deletes the post. Too late. So now he or she has to come up with a way to cover the embarrassment. What is the first thing the athlete says? "My account was hacked." As if everything is okay and people will believe that noise. Nope. No one believes it. So what is the next step? The athlete shuts down his or her social media account or all of them. Now the athlete looks even more guilty. Why? Well, if the account were truly hacked, then the hacker would be in control of the account, so the hacker should still be posting bad things under the athlete's name until the athlete could contact the help desk gurus of the social media platform to have it shut down.

Of course, when someone has posted something inappropriate, the other excuse is "Someone else had access to my account, it wasn't me." No one is believing that one either. Why? Because it begs the question, why would you let someone have access to your account? That doesn't make sense. Did you give someone your phone? Why would you give your phone to someone who would post inappropriate things on your behalf? I have even heard the excuse "My phone was stolen." Well, I have had my phone stolen as well, but I never had anyone post dumb things on my behalf in my social media. As a matter of fact, as soon as my phone was stolen, I got online and had my phone provider lock my phone down immediately. You see, these are excuses. You are not fooling anyone with them. It only makes you look worse. Your best bet is to own your mistakes. Take responsibility. Apologize and make amends where you can. Move on. That will make your errors go away faster than any excuse will.

MYTH 5: SOCIAL MEDIA IS MY BUSINESS, NOT YOURS

Actually, social media is everyone's business—that's the social part. You posted it. You made it fodder for public consumption. Among your friends, fans, and cheerleaders are predators ready to pounce. You may say and even think that your social media is your business, but it's public. Sure, the situation is not fair, but that is not the point. When you post something, you voluntarily give up control of it. You don't know what happens to what you post after you post it—where it goes, who sees it, who reposts it for what reasons with what new spin. Just assume that your private life is over once you use social media. Your business is now everyone's playground.

MYTH 6: I HAVE FREEDOM OF SPEECH, SO I CAN SAY AND DO WHAT I WANT

You do have freedom of speech, which protects you from government reprisals resulting from what you say, but it does not protect you from the swift consequences experienced in social media environments. Every action, whether it is physical behavior, words that you say, or words that you type, comes with consequences: positive, negative, or sometimes both. Although you are certainly free to say anything you want, you cannot control how it is received. The safest bet is to keep things positive or say nothing at all. Unfortunately, people will forget much of the good that you do, but they will be quick to remember nearly all of your past transgressions. Cardale Jones may go on to do a lot of great things in the NFL, but he will live the rest of his life as the guy who went to college but only wanted to play football and not go to class. Yes, you can say whatever it is that you want, but that does not exempt you from the consequences.

THE BREAK DOWN

There are number of myths when it comes to social media and athletes. Some myths have elements of truth to them, but most of them are just myths and simply not true. Ask yourself about which myths you believe about social media. Are you believing one of the myths that I have mentioned, or maybe you are all in on one I did not write down that can inhibit you from being as effective as possible when it comes to your social media use? Do not believe something about social media because other people do something on social media and appear to get away with it. No one is truly getting away with anything on social media. This may be the biggest myth of all. Depending on how you use your voice on social media, your posts can pay you back or be used against you. It is ultimately your choice. Choose wisely, and choose positively.

3

YOUR BRAND ON SOCIAL MEDIA

Some of you may say, "Social media? Why analyze it so deeply? Who cares?" The fact is that social media is really important in our society. It is no longer a fad. It is a part of our daily lives. Half of all Internet users are using social media. Facebook alone has over 1.5 billion users worldwide. Social media is now the number one way in which news is broken and reported, trends are created, and reputations are ruined. Social media is real—yes, it will evolve over time, but it is here to stay.

Not only is social media here to stay, but people are especially interested in what athletes and celebrities are saying. However, when you become an athlete who achieves a certain level of success in any sport, your life is not your own anymore. By accepting that scholarship or joining your team, you traded your identity as an individual athlete for that of a teammate. You are now part of a larger group and represent that group, its coaches, the athletic program, and the school. What you do is no longer just about you. You are part of a fraternity or sorority of athletes that has a history and a future. Part of that bond you will forever have is the understanding that you need to respect and appreciate the position you have been given as a result of your talent. Responsibility comes with that privilege.

You may be a golfer at a state school in a small town, but say something on social media about how you don't have enough time to practice your sport because of all the studying you have to do, and you will have reinforced people's stereotype of how athletes expect a free ride to play their sport without having to go to class and earn good grades. Of course, we know that plenty of student athletes work hard at both their sport and their studies; however, the general public doesn't know what we know. Even when you try to educate people who believe in the myth of the coasting college athlete, they often don't believe your testimony, anyway. Besides, now they've got evidence from social media backing up their point. This is why it becomes all the more important to continually do the right thing, say the right thing, and be the right person on your social media.

HOW DOES SOCIAL MEDIA BRAND ME?

When you see the Nike Swoosh, you immediately know what it is. The word *Nike* doesn't have to appear anywhere near the Swoosh; we all know it represents Nike. What does this have to do with you? The fact is, even before you attended your college or university, you were creating your brand through social media. Think about the different posts, snaps, grams, and tweets you have thrown into cyberspace. What does your social media say about your brand? Is it a brand that everyone wants to be a part of, or is it a brand that people want to stay away from?

Everything you put on social media represents something about you—something you find funny, something you think is important, something that's on your mind. When people see a series of snippets of your life and thoughts, they get a sense of who you are and what you're about; in other words, they start to get a picture of you. That picture is your brand. If I were to look at your social media for as little as five minutes, I could tell you your brand. I would learn about your intelligence, your self-control, your ability to communicate, your positivity, your negativity, what's important to you, your focus, your interests, and the type of people that you surround yourself with, among other things. Taken together, your social media output ultimately tells people if they can trust the brand. That brand is you.

You may be surprised that I use the word *trust*. However, what you are doing with your social media now is creating a brand that your future employers can trust. Whether you go into professional sports or become a professional in another field, your future employers will want to know that they can trust you. Developing your brand in the right way on social media can help develop trust before you embark on your first career after college.

You may think that developing trust in you and your brand is not that big of a deal right now. It is. Coaches, administrators, the sports media, parents, alumni, and future employers are paying attention to what you are posting on social media. Ask yourself, "What is the message I want to give people?" What opinion do you want people to have of you? The beauty of social media is that you have complete control over what you share. If you focus on being positive and proactive with your social media, it will help put you in a much better position for your next career.

PENALTY BOX, STRIKEOUTS, AND DISQUALIFICATIONS

Certain topics and subjects, if they continually pop up on your social media, will affect your brand both now and in the future. Continue to post troublesome things and you might find that you have no future. Here are some of the content themes that have caused the most problems for student athletes:

► Sexually related content
► Alcohol-related content
► Drug-related content
► Racially charged content
► Politically charged content
► Verbal abuse of anyone
► Hazing of any type
► Profanity
► Violence of any type
► Negative talk about school, the university, coaches, or teammates

Of course, there are plenty of additional categories of potentially offensive posts; this list hits some of the biggest targets. The takeaway here is to think through what you are considering posting and use your common sense.

YOUR BRAND STARTS NOW

You will be a professional in some field when you get older. Perhaps you will be among the elite few who make it to the next level in your sport. What is more likely is that you will be a professional in some other career. Regardless of what the future holds, social media can haunt you or help you: it can literally make or break your brand. Think about how a post may send ripples into your future before you send your thoughts to the Internet today.

Brand consistency, also known as *brand integrity*, is important, and given that you've got your eye on the future, you need to start laying the groundwork now. What that means is that you should be building a great brand on social media by saying fun, entertaining, positive, and neutral things. Believe me, people are paying attention. Consistently good-natured social media posts tell others, including your future employer, that you are smart, fun, witty, entertaining, and have a positive attitude—all things that any employer would want in a future employee.

Then there is the other side, when you send out a tweet, snap, or gram that is abusive, filled with profanity, sexually charged, or made up of references to controlled substances—in short, your social media post demonstrates bad judgment. Because people—remember your next employer?—are watching, they are going to see what you've posted and question whether you are a safe person to hire, whether they can trust you if something goes wrong or you get mad. Now it becomes difficult to overcome what you said, because you posted it, the Internet immortalized it, and they have read it. This is why you have to consider every single thing you put out there.

I am often hired by companies to look at prospective employees. Many times, I am investigating young women and men who are right out of college. Regardless of the position the candidates have applied for, the first thing I do is look at all of their social media profiles. I want to see each prospective employee's brand on social media. Depending on what I see, I make a recommendation regarding whether the company should hire this person. These candidates, wittingly or unwittingly, have already created their brand; my job is to determine if the brand a job candidate has created on social media can coexist with the brand image of the company. Whether you go on to be a professional athlete who may be asked to endorse a product or service or you switch fields to work for that company in sales or management, your social media history affects your brand, and your brand, in turn, affects whether you will be chosen to represent a particular company. Let me show you how companies look at your social media so you can better understand how what you post affects your job prospects.

First, how private are your profiles? When companies see your social media profiles are private, it raises a red flag for them. It makes them wonder what are you hiding and why you are hiding it. This is especially true for an athlete who has had a lot of interaction with the public. A company will pass over a candidate with a private profile for one with a profile that is public and positive. So often you will hear people telling you to make your profiles private. As someone who is hired by companies to profile, select, and hire candidates, social media is where I start. If I cannot access a profile, I am hesitant to bring a candidate in for an interview. I want people who use social media and use it in a positive way. This is because the companies that I work for typically see their employees as advertisements for their company. They know the right image online can only help their bottom line.

Think of your social media history as being like a credit history. If you do not have a history of credit, it is very difficult to get future credit. By the same token, if you have a history of bad credit, well, good luck trying to get more credit when you need it. However, if you have a great credit history, you can get more credit when you really need it. Be aware that if you mess up your credit, depending on how bad the situation is, you will have a difficult time rebuilding your credit. The same is true with social media. You are building social capital. That social capital can have a positive effect on your future, especially your financial future, when it comes to obtaining and maintaining your future career. If you lack social capital, it is going to be an unnecessarily difficult uphill climb.

Second, how positive is your social media? What do your social media profiles on the different platforms say about you? That is, do you portray a positive image or a negative one? If someone went through your profiles on different platforms, would that person get the sense that you will be a positive influence in the workplace? For example, if your Instagram posts are filled with fun, positive, enjoyable experiences versus experiences that are morally or ethically questionable, the company will be more attracted to you as a job candidate.

Third, how well have you promoted yourself? Companies want to see the strategies you use to present yourself to the world. After all, if you have done a good job at projecting a positive image, that tells human resources that you have the potential to promote their company. Social media is incredibly powerful when it comes to brands and companies. If you use social media in the right way, you demonstrate that you have successfully promoted yourself by having high follower counts, and high interaction makes you extremely attractive to future employers.

I want to give you a social media tip that your professors and other students probably do not know: start building your LinkedIn profile now. You may or may not be familiar with LinkedIn, the professional social media network. Think of it as a place where people find jobs, exchange ideas about companies and careers, and connect with others to help grow their businesses. This platform, of all the social media platforms, has the highest percentage of educated and wealthy people participating.

Chances are, if you are looking for a job out of college, the person who is going to hire you or the CEO of the company you are interested in has a profile on LinkedIn. First, these profiles can be sources of information about the places you want to work and the people who are already there. But second, the profiles of successful professionals you're hoping to join in the workplace are terrific sources of ideas regarding formatting and details to include in your own profile. Follow their lead while adding your own personal touches as you build your own LinkedIn page. There may not be much on it to start, but perhaps you have an idea of what you would like to do in the future. Add your coursework, volunteer work, and the other things that you are involved with right now as a student athlete that help to build a credible, well-rounded LinkedIn profile.

Double Bonus Box: Getting Your First Job in Your Career through LinkedIn

Here is a bonus secret about LinkedIn that very few people are aware of: Did you know that there is a place on LinkedIn where you can find internships in your field, as well as your first career position, and your only competition is other students like you? It's true! If you go to https://students.linkedin.com, you can learn about how to create a great LinkedIn profile, what you should consider when building the profile, and career opportunities. You will be happy to also know that they have an app for both iPhone and Android that will make it far more convenient for you to check out internships and jobs. I have recommended this for many college students, and it has led to tremendous success for them. I believe you will achieve great things with it, too.

Finally, I want to talk to you about your brand when it comes to your family. When you are on social media, chances are that many of your family members do not have a clue about what you are doing. There are several reasons for this. Sometimes it is because they are older or not plugged in and they do not have social media accounts. Sometimes it is because you have blocked them from seeing your accounts. Sometimes it is because you are using a specific social media platform that they have not taken the time to learn. And sometimes your family may just not want to know what you do on social media. Yet even if your family isn't on or following you on social media, here is one sure thing: if you say something really wrong in the social media realm, they will hear about it.

Before you were an athlete and long after you have left your sport, the first team you belonged to and the last team you will belong to is your family. Your actions reflect on them as much as they reflect on you. Even if Mom doesn't stumble across your inappropriate social media material herself, you can count on a family friend—or should I say, "friend"—telling your mom, dad, or grandmother about what you said on social media, perhaps accompanying the revelation with a sly look that clearly indicates the friend is speculating about whether that view you expressed was one you got from home. Yes, your bad behavior can also brand your family. It goes deeper. Although you may think that your rant is not a big deal, the people who raised you are going to be asking themselves, "Where did I go wrong?"

Sit with that a moment: your family will not so much blame you as they will blame themselves. They will be the ones to live with the pain and embarrassment of something you said or posted. They will want it to go away. It will not. While you are in school, insulated by your studies, your coach, and your team, they will be living with the questions they ask themselves or field from others: "Why did he/she say that?" "Why did he/she do that?" There is no escape for them. Is it fair? That is an interesting question, because so much of life is not fair. However, it is just one more consequence of a bad action on social media that leads to bad branding that affects more than just you. Never forget that you are always representing your family's brand.

4

SOCIAL MEDIA HOME RUNS AND FOUL BALLS

I know that you are tired of hearing about what not to do on social media. Frankly, so am I! Coming at social media from the angle of what not to do often makes one look right past the fact that social media can be used in a positive way to help you now and in your future. In this section, I explore some of those positive strategies, as well as some traps to avoid. A number of the things I am about to mention here may sound like common sense, but perhaps they will also help you think about social media in a different way.

HOME RUNS
1. BE PART OF SOCIAL MEDIA
Look, it's fun. Your friends are there. The media is there. Your future is there, too. Just do it the right way. Post respectfully and share consciously. There are many benefits to social media if you manage it properly.

2. DO GOOD THINGS FOR PEOPLE ON SOCIAL MEDIA
Support and encourage people through social media. Keep it positive. Be inspirational. Be funny (in a good way). En-

courage your teammates. Promote a local charity with your social media. Do good, not harm.

3. GIVE YOUR FUTURE EMPLOYERS OR SPONSORS FOOD FOR THOUGHT

If you want to stay in the sports world or any business world, for that matter, after your college career ends, then use social media as a tool to let your future sponsors and employers know what kind of person you are. If you want to go into sports broadcasting, for example, demonstrate some of your skills. Create a YouTube channel to show people what you know and what you can do by sharing your thoughts in an entertaining or original way. Give people your insights on your favorite subject, whether it is business, physics, math, engineering, Renaissance art, or something more esoteric. You can use YouTube to build a video resume before you even get to your career. If you are good on camera and social media, you can give your future career an extra boost!

4. ASK FOR FEEDBACK ABOUT YOUR SOCIAL MEDIA

I am not saying you have to do this all the time. However, occasionally ask one or more of your adult friends—maybe a coach, an administrator, or someone who will tell you the truth about what he or she thinks—how they think you are doing on social media. Ask them if you are getting too close to the line. Ask if there is a better way to say this or that. Ask if you should say something at all. Heck, ask me! I would be happy to tell you how you could express yourself on social media better and more productively than you are currently. The point is, every now and then, check in with a trusted someone to ensure your social media message is staying on target.

5. TAKE A BREAK

Sometimes you need to unplug from social media. This may surprise you, but I highly recommend it. Maybe do it during your season. Maybe do it during the off-season. The timing is up to you, but do take a break from all of it occasionally. Clear your head. Give yourself some space. It really is okay to step away from all of the noise. Look, this is my career. But every now and then, even I have to shut my social media down and go dark for a while. Sometimes you need to do it for a few days; sometimes you may need a break of a few weeks. Whatever duration you choose is really OK. You are not hurting your brand by temporarily disengaging. Granted, it is not easy to do. I can assure you, though, that after a few days of not worrying about your social media, you actually feel less pressure to be on social media. I know it will be difficult, but do it. I promise, life will look different and yet still be amazing without it, even for a short period of time.

FOUL BALLS

1. BEING SHORTSIGHTED LEADS TO GETTING BLINDSIDED

It might seem cool to say something snarky about your coach, your school, or other teammates, but it is not. It could cost you your future. You thought you wanted to be a broadcaster after college should you not go pro in your sport? Forget about it. Your nasty tweets, snaps, and grams will haunt you and keep you out of the media.

2. DON'T BE BAITED

People are waiting to bait you into an argument, a political discussion, or a stupid comment about your rival. Don't fall for it. Before social media, there were these things called newspapers. We have all been told or seen stories of players from a rival team saying something disparaging about another team and bragging to some reporter about how they were going to beat us into the ground. As is typical the reporter, who may or may not have goaded them into talking smack got what he or she wanted . . . a story. Of course, the reporter writes the story, uses the quotes from the player and then it gets printed in a local newspaper, on TV or social media. I recall situations like this happening in football and the guys on the team purchasing multiple copies of the printed paper. At that time, we had a bulletin board in the locker room. I recall a time when the who board was covered the with numerous copies of the headlines and specific statements. The inflammatory text served as extra motivation to feul our drive to shove those words right back down their throats. I even remember some guys having the quotes taped to their ankles. You know how talking smack often backfires? Most of the time. And it all started with a reporter baiting a player to say something about their opponent they should have never said.

3. DON'T GET DEFENSIVE

When you have people talking trash about you and yours, no matter how negative it is, no matter which member of the family they want to pick on, you cannot get defensive. You cannot retaliate. Regardless of what the haters say, your best defense is to ignore the chatter. Move on. I am not saying it will be easy. It is not easy for me, even as a grown adult, when someone does it. Leave it alone and, given enough time, one of two things happens: either someone with much higher authority or knowledge will have your back or it goes away. I have said this over and over: if you want to get rid of the trolls, don't feed them! You will never win by responding in kind. They take on no risk in taunting you, and they know it. They just want to bring you down to their level, so stay above it.

TAKE A TIME-OUT AND WIN

I have a very simple, very effective technique to help reduce the risk of things going bad on social media. It is called "Take a Time-Out and WIN." Here is how it works.

TAKE A TIME-OUT

Before you hit that button on your phone to post, gram, snap, or tweet, call a time-out. Take thirty seconds. Reread what you wrote, look at the video again, examine the foreground and the background in that photo, and even do it again. Ask yourself, "Do I really want to post this?" If there is any hesitation at all in your mind, don't push the button. You are an athlete, so you know that a time-out gives you the opportunity to regroup and ensure you have a workable plan going forward. Similarly, make sure before anything goes out into the social media cybersphere that your post is part of a good plan. How do you make sure of this? I'm glad you asked, because that means you're ready to WIN.

W—WWGT = WHAT WOULD YOUR GRANDMOTHER THINK?

This is the safest way to put it. If your grandmother would think what you are about to post is bad, then don't post it. If your grandmother would be proud, go with it. If your grandmother wouldn't understand it? Well, then maybe you need to be a bit more clear in your social media post.

I—INTENTIONAL

Do everything you do with intention. What does that mean? Simply put, don't just throw stuff out there on your social media. When you post, really think about what you are saying. Deeply consider what exactly you are writing and how other people may view it. Analyze that picture or video and try to figure out what it might represent to someone who doesn't share your background or experiences. Every word you put down, every picture you are thinking of posting, do it with a purpose. Do not post just to post. Be able to truthfully say to yourself, "I know what I am posting here and why I am posting it, and this will not hurt my future."

N—NOW

The last part of WIN is *now*. That is, after considering whether this is going to be in the best interest of your brand, your team, and your family and being absolutely intentional about every word or picture you are about to post, ask yourself, is now the time to post it? Maybe it meets all of the criteria—it's good, it's cool, it's safe. If that's the case, then no worries: push the button with a clear conscience. However, maybe now is not the time. Maybe it is halftime and you need to rethink what you're doing. Maybe your post is something to save for later. Maybe a different time would be ideal. Make sure you always know when your best time to post is. Moments move fast; it's okay if your now comes later.

5

PLAYING OFFENSE

Let's turn now to offense. As an athlete, you know better than most that you cannot win if you do not score points. So how does one score points when it comes to using social media? Because you are in a place where you are setting up your future career, scoring points for your future is important. Understand that scoring in social media is not the same as putting points on the board, nor is anyone going to give you a medal for everything you post. However, when you are doing the things I suggest, over time, you will be putting yourself in a winning position when it comes to your future career, and the feedback you receive will indicate that you are on track. Someone will write or stop to tell you that something you shared online had a positive effect on them; a coach, future employer, or a fan will tell you they think you're doing a great job. You will be banking points and building your social capital for your successful future and staying on track for your great present as well.

In this chapter, I offer suggestions for how you can better ensure that you have a positive impact with your social media use and avoid the pitfalls that you have so often heard about. I know that when you first look at what I have suggested, it may sound a bit lame or old school, but you also need to begin understanding that you are only a few short years from becoming a professional in some business or going to graduate school. I am not saying you have to do the things I mention in the following section with every post, but you should rotate these social media plays in as part of your social media presence. You will be not only surprised by how much difference it makes, but your future career will be thanking you for it.

THE VOLUNTEER PLAY

You may do this already, but chances are, as an athlete, you are going to be asked to volunteer for a charity. If the charity aligns with your values, say yes! You don't have to say yes to every charity that asks and overextend yourself, but pick one or two or three that you love. Use the opportunity to help others by taking pictures, recording videos, and writing about the charity and sharing all of this material on social media. Express what you admire about the charity, why you support it, and what you and others can do for it. You are in a position as an athlete to raise awareness about an issue in a way that can help a charity and, by extension, everyone and everything the charity serves. Use your power of attracting attention to help. Regularly bring up the charity and show your interaction with the people who run it as well as with those whom the charity helps. There are many great causes in your local area and just as many ways to help. A prime example is a visit to a children's hospital. I promise you, your willingness to spend time with hospitalized kids will mean a great deal to them. This is a great play for you and your social media.

THE AWAY GAME

As an athlete, you get to do something that a typical college student does not get to do regularly during the school year: travel. So post about it! You may not think traveling is a big deal, but to many people, it is a huge deal. Why is this? A psychologist might tell you that there are two reasons. First, people are curious. Second, people like to travel, literally and figuratively, through the lives of others. Have you ever noticed how many shows there are about eating and traveling and traveling in general? Entire TV stations are devoted to showing viewers other parts of the country or world. Why? Because, as humans, we are interested in the novel, we dream, we consider whether this exotic-to-us locale is a place we want to go. People—not just family and friends, but strangers and fans—want to accompany you on your travels and see the world through your eyes. You will find that not only will your travel posts get more likes and comments than your posts from home, but people will share your posts about your travels, too.

THE SELFIE WEFIE STRATEGY

What? Selfies? Yes, selfies and wefies. In case you are not acquainted with *wefies*, it is a term for group selfies. Yes, people do like selfies and wefies. You take them anyway, so make sure to take a few while you are in your uniform. Take them with your teammates. Take them with your fans. Then post away! Yes, I know they may seem to project an image that you are a bit narcissistic, but selfies and wefies are a fun part of social media. So keep your clothes on—remember, bonus points if you're wearing your uniform!—and shoot some pictures of you, you and your teammates, and you and your coaches. Do not feel like your pictures always have to be serious. They can be silly, intense, or somewhere in between. Humans really like seeing other humans having fun. So show us the fun side of you and your sport!

THE DOCUMENTARY PLAY

Previously, I told you about the away game. You can take it a step further to what I call the *documentary play*. Humans are interested in what others do, not just where they go. Many people think that being a college athlete is easy. They believe, wrongly, that you live this plush life, do not have to attend class, and find life to be smooth sailing. Want to correct that impression? Show people what it is really like. Create a video demonstrating a day in the life of a student athlete: waking up exhausted, going to the training room before breakfast to get treatment, grabbing a quick bite to eat, rushing to class, taking notes, going to practice, finding the time to study, finals week, and so on. For a great example, check out Wisconsin Badger Nigel Hayes's Hayes for Days series, episodes of which are posted on the Wisconsin Badgers YouTube channel. He is creative and funny, and he really gives a glimpse of college life. Plus, he does it in such a real way that you can tell he is having fun, too.

But you're not limited to showing people an average day in the life of a student athlete. Perhaps you can shoot a video that takes viewers through what happens before a game and how you prepare. Everyone is interested in fitness today, so show us your workout. Perhaps, as an athlete, you eat differently than most people do. Share it! You never know what your reporting will lead to. You may end up owning your own gym or restaurant, working in the health and nutrition field, or perhaps being a spokesperson for a major franchise. Your documentaries may even lead to a television career. By making this play through video, you could jump-start a career that will be waiting for you when you finish college.

JUST ONE EXAMPLE OF A GREAT OFFENSE

Marcus Paige played basketball for the University of North Carolina. He and the North Carolina Tar Heels fell short in the 2016 National Championship game against Villanova, losing on a last-second shot at the end of regulation time. However, if you want to see an example of someone who has played great social media offense, go to Marcus Paige's Twitter profile: @marcuspaige5. He talks about all sorts of subjects, takes pictures and videos, and is having a great time on Twitter. He has over 324,000 followers at the time of this writing, and I expect that number will only go up, whether he ultimately ends up in the NBA, on television as a sports commentator, or elsewhere for what is sure to be a stellar professional career. His use of social media is making him a star, right now for the Alt Lake City Stars NBA D-League, but it could just as well be company who would love to have them as part of their brand. Just take a moment to look through his Twitter posts for a great example of someone who has played at an incredibly high level both on the court and in social media. Here are few examples of things he wrote:

- ► 14 Oct 2015 Fall Break coming through at the perfect time! Needed a few days off from the grind
- ► 27 Sep 2015 Too early for Christmas music? Or nah
- ► 20 Jul 2015 Shoutout @ZachJohnsonPGA for winning the Open! Representing Iowa at the highest level

As you can see it just a few examples he talks about a variety of subjects, and he posts a variety of pictures of fans wearing his numbers, or seeing him at the local burger place, but all of it is authentic, positive, and makes puts him in a great position for his future, regardless of what that may be.

6

PLAYING DEFENSE

You have most likely heard it said that defense wins championships. It's true: if the other team can't score, you can't lose. Playing defense on social media can keep you from losing as well, whether that loss be in the form of playing time, a scholarship, or your future career. The defensive plays that follow can keep you from losing and will prevent someone else from scoring on you.

GAME LOSS ZONE DEFENSE

One of the things I really love about Marcus Paige's Twitter feed is that he did not post after North Carolina lost to Villanova. That was a smart defensive move. We all know that after a loss, especially a critical loss like in a championship game, we are likely to feel emotional. After all, as I stated before, as an athlete, you are competitive. The pain of losing hurts, and it hurts more than winning feels good. You hate it. Every athlete does. Knowing that, be aware that when you are in that angry, hurt, want-to-scream-at-the-world-how-you-feel zone, you need to play defense on social media and not post.

Not posting while emotional is a great play for a variety of reasons. First, there are people who love to kick other people when they are down or angry. There's even a psychological term for the phenomenon: it's called *schadenfreude*—gaining pleasure from other people's misery or pain. Trust me, people who experience schadenfreude are out there. You may think of them as trolls, haters, or worse, but they are looking for an athlete to lose and post about it so they can rub the loss in the player's face. Yes, it is cruel. I wish I could tell you that this is the modus operandi of just a few unkind people, but the fact is that you must assume millions of them are out there just waiting for an opportunity to make fun of you or kick you when you are down. When you are in that painful zone, play the defense of not posting.

THE CORNER BLITZ

The corner blitz occurs when out of nowhere, someone who thinks that he or she is clever rips into you, your family, your team, your teammate, your coach, or your school. You never saw it coming. All of sudden, BAM! A post nearly knocks the wind out of you. Because it is so personal, the unanticipated slam leaves you stunned and angry. In response to such un-called-for aggression, you must do what you do on the field when you get hit hard by your opponent. Get up. Walk away. Move on to the next play. Above all, do not let the poster know you are hurt. By not responding, you rob the poster of the satisfaction of knowing that he or she got to you. Seriously, the best revenge is to move on. In case I have not been clear, I'll say it again: leave it alone. Remember what I told you earlier: if you don't feed the trolls, they will die.

TEAM DEFENSE

There may be times during your season that your teammates and coaches jointly decide that all of you are going to turn off social media. I call this *team defense*, because you are not making this decision as an individual; you are making this decision as part of a team to avoid any possible distractions that can occur as a result of one team member's social media posts. This defense is typically mandated by coaches, but occasionally it is decided by a majority group vote by the team.

A great example of this is the University of Connecticut's (UConn's) women's basketball team. UConn's women's basketball is a dominant force in Division 1 college sports. They have won ten national championships since 2000 and four consecutive championships since 2013, including the 2016 National Championship. Part of their success might be attributable to the fact that Twitter is shut down for the team from the first day of practice to the final day of the season. Typically, the day before practice, the UConn women announce on their Twitter accounts something to the effect of "See ya later, Twitter." That may seem extreme to you, but, in fact, if you ask these champion athletes, they will tell you that the Twitter blackout is a good thing. It is one less thing to think about and allows them to have a better focus on what they need to do on the court with fewer distractions.

At first glance, you may think this Twitter blackout is drastic and unnecessary. However, as I noted before, taking a break from your social media can be helpful, giving you a chance to get centered or just inhabit a quiet space in which you can recharge your mental batteries. You may feel like you need to be on social media all the time, but you really do not. As a matter of fact, you will likely find that the longer you do not use social media, the less stress you feel and the more you engage with your teammates and coaches. I can understand that you may want to argue against it; however, it's hard to argue with four national championships in a row.

There are teams in other sports that do the same thing. For example, Clemson University football players are not allowed to post on social media during the season. Not everyone likes that policy, and they certainly do not all agree with it, but that is part of being on that team. Just because we do not like or agree with something doesn't mean it is the wrong thing to do. In fact, it may be turn out to be the best thing for the team.

DEACTIVATION DEFENSE

Laremy Tunsil played left tackle for the University of Mississippi. He was projected to be the first offensive lineman to be selected in the 2016 NFL draft. At one point, he was predicted to be the first pick overall.

Thirty minutes before the draft started, a video was shared on his Twitter timeline of him with a gas mask on, smoking a bowl of marijuana. He admitted the video was of him, but he added the caveat that it was recorded when he was younger. His value immediately dropped among the NFL teams interested in him. Not only was he not the top draft pick, Tunsil was not even among the top ten.

On the bright side, Tunsil was still picked in the first round. However, the video cost him money and future endorsements. He is going to have to spend who knows how long trying to prove to coaches, teammates, fans, and the media that he does not have off-the-field issues. He is on the proverbial short leash: if he does anything else questionable, he is not going to get the benefit of the doubt. Even though the video was out for less than a couple of minutes, it was quickly saved and reposted all over the Internet by every major news outlet and plenty of individuals. His defensive move of temporarily deactivating his social media accounts was a great one: it kept people from posting on his accounts while at the same time preventing him from seeing and responding to the negativity, potentially making things even worse.

If you do have to deactivate, the question I am commonly asked is, "For how long?" There is no clear answer to this question. Some athletes have been know to deactivate for a month or two to a year or two, and some have never reactivated their social media accounts. Deactivation sounds severe, but it is a great defensive move that lets you remain under the radar, stay out of the news, and dodge any (or any more) trouble. It really is the safest defensive play in the playbook. If you think that anything in your past could come back to haunt you in your future, then running the deactivation defense may be the play for you.

CONCLUSION: PREGAME GOALS THAT LEAD TO A WIN

I know that when it comes to any athletic competition, we set goals. Some are more specific than others. Some are for the entire season, and some are for each game. Social media is really no different. Every day you are on social media, you are, in fact, in competition with yourself and perhaps others. You have to compete against your emotions, the way you feel physically, the stress, the duality of being a student and an athlete and more. Each day is game day. It starts when you get up in the morning, and the final buzzer sounds when you finally go to sleep at night. In between those times, you will have to make choices about what you are going to post. Being clear about what you are going to do is going to help ensure that you will have the best chance at getting the win each and every day.

WHAT SHOULD MY SOCIAL MEDIA GOALS BE?
When I thought about this section heading, my thoughts immediately went back to the meetings my team would have just prior to going out on the field during my play-

ing days. My coach, Tom Hood, would list our goals for the game: how many points we would give up, how many yards we would gain, the number of turnovers we were to get, and so on. However, the last goal was exactly the same for every game: have fun. Rather than ending with that, I am starting this list with it. The first goal you should have is to have fun with social media. Be social. Interact. Enjoy it. You can do that without being crude, rude, or inappropriate in some manner. Interact with people in a positive way. Talk, laugh, share: this communication device was meant to provide fun, first and foremost.

The second goal is to remain positive. If you have nothing good to say, don't say it. This does not mean you cannot have a bad day. In fact, if your chemistry class is difficult, it is okay to say, "Man, chemistry is hard." We get it, because for some of us, including me, chemistry is hard. If you are not feeling well, it's okay to say, "I hate having the flu." That is not the kind of negativity I am talking about. I am talking about posting something that could be construed as hurtful, whining, mean-spirited, abusive, profane, or the like. You may feel like saying something cutting out of spite, frustration, or anger, but doing so is only going to make things worse. Rewrite those emotionally charged statements into a more acceptable form or do not say anything at all. The fact is, no one—I mean absolutely no one—can troll you or shame you if you stay positive on social media. They may try, but in the end, only they will look foolish.

Your third goal is to use social media with the future in view. Think about how you can use social media so well that you are putting yourself in the best possible position to be successful after college. Employers are searching people's social media to see what they have done and can do. Give your future employers something that excites them. Give them something that strengthens their confidence in you. Give them the social media output that convinces them to put their trust in you! As I said earlier, you control your social media. When you control your social media in the right way, you are opening doors to your future that you are not even thinking about right now. You got this!

HOW MUCH TIME SHOULD YOU SPEND ON SOCIAL MEDIA?

There is no right or wrong answer here. According to the Fieldhouse Media research, the majority of you spend about an hour per day on social media. If it is not inhibiting you from being successful in the classroom or on the field or court, then I think the amount of time is up to you. Just know that some people can handle less or more, depending on their habits. The key here is to make sure that your social media is enhancing rather than interfering with your success.

I do believe you will find that if you reduce the amount of time you use social media or do not use social media at all while in season, you will have a much easier time focusing on school and your sport. I recognize, though, that reducing your social media use is difficult. You will need to maintain a disciplined schedule. For example, you may want to intentionally leave your phone in your dorm room during a class or two. (I know that sent shivers down your spine as soon as you read it, but sometimes the ends justify the means!) Another strategy is to turn your phone on silent. Not vibrate, not a low ring tone, not flashing—complete silence. You will be surprised by how much less you will refer to your social media when your phone isn't prompting you to do so with dings and buzzes.

In all likelihood, you have created habits with how you check your social media. You may have even become predictable. I am willing to bet that you have checked your phone at some point while reading this section. Of course, the easiest way to cut down on your social media use is to take a step beyond the silent strategy I just suggested and instead turn your phone off. I know this sounds like blasphemy! However, because we tend to have a phone with us at all times and because most of us are constantly getting notifications on that phone (e.g., texts, e-mail dings, and social media notifications), it can be nearly impossible to stop checking them. Turning off your phone and checking your notifications later actually is a safer way to go. You are cringing at the thought, aren't you? That's normal. When someone is asked to do something he or she doesn't want to do, there is an immediate psychological reactance or, in other words, an opposite internal reaction that resists doing it. Even so, I am confident that your will is stronger than your initial reluctance.

This leads me to another point about human psychology that most people emotionally struggle with, although intellectually they know it is true. That is, when we try to mentally and emotionally focus on more than one task at the same time, it is not possible to give any one task full attention, nor is it possible to perform at the highest level on any one of the tasks. Social media is one more thing that can take away our focus or, at the very least, distract us from giving our best performance. As a student athlete, you have so many balls to juggle as it is. Adding one more ball to your juggling act, no matter how small or seemingly insignificant it may be, can make your other tasks that much more difficult. When checking your phone and reading a notification from one of your social media platforms, it can be nearly impossible to hear anything else: everything else in the world shuts off. You only hear in your head the words that are being read because, most likely, they are about you. Meanwhile, something important could have been happening, but you missed it. Most people think they can do two things at the same time, yet according to the National Safety Council, one out of four car accidents is caused by some sort of texting while driving.[4] The point is, be stronger than social media and avoid the distractions that are keeping you from being the best student and the best athlete you can be.

THE FINAL BUZZER

Social media is a great tool. However, you also need to understand that some people use this tool as a weapon. Weapons, in this case, are not used to help; they are only used to hurt. You need to use social media to help your career, school, and family reputation. Here's a quick recap on how to use social media as a tool to help you while protecting yourself from missteps and those who wield social media as a weapon.

First, before we get started, remember that social media is fun. I mean it—I want you to have fun with it! Your college career is going to be filled with hard work, but it also should be filled with people, activities, events, and adventures that you will always remember with a smile. This is a great time of your life, one that you will never get back once you leave school. Enjoy it. Live it. Document it. Use social media in an entertaining way that takes us with you on your journey. Let us experience it with you.

Look, I know that you cannot play your sport at a high level if you are not somewhat emotional. However, do not let your emotions control your social media posts. When I teach psychology and I talk about emotions, I talk about emotional control and emotional intelligence. In other words, I talk about how you can control your emotions. I give the following example: If you kick me in the shin, I do not have to kick you or hit you back. I could curl up in a ball and cry. I could laugh at you. I could simply walk away. That is, I have a choice when it comes to my emotional reactions. We all have that choice. You do not have to react in an inappropriate way. Take emotional control and demonstrate your emotional intelligence by using social media without anger, malice, or inappropriate pictures or language.

Be a team player when it comes to social media. You are not alone. Your teammates surround you, and you have to work together to be successful. So often we hear in sports about "playing the game the right way"—this means, in essence, playing as a team. When you leave the practice field or court or when the game is over, you are still part of a team. Even when you are not around teammates, you are still part of the team. Whatever you do outside of the team still has an effect on your team. If you do the right thing on social media, you and your team will have no worries and no problems. If you do the wrong thing on social media, the distraction starts, worry begins, and, depending on what is posted, problems will arise.

Do the right thing by your coaches when using social media. When I played in college, some of my coaches became like bonu's parents, but most were mentors. They helped me grow up. They helped guide me to my next career after college. They were important to me. Like you, I did not always agree with their decisions, but, then again, I didn't agree with my parents all the time, either. But I do know that all of them, parents and coaches alike, were doing their best to help me. Every one of you, whether you are a walk-on or a full-scholarship athlete, can have a positive or negative effect on your coaches simply by what you post on your social media. I promise you, your coaches worked hard to get where they are now. You can help them maintain their gains by doing the right thing on social media.

Think, too, about your school when you post on social media. This may seem like a weird thing to say, but as a student athlete, you do represent something much bigger than you or even your team: you represent your college or university. That school has given you an opportunity to play your sport beyond high school. I know you have heard it said that less than 2 percent of you will go on to play your sport professionally. This means that for more than 98 percent of you, this is it when it comes to sports. However, your degree is going to be carried with you forever. You will always be a representative of your college. Use your social media in a way that makes your college a place that companies and businesses want to look to, to find their next hire, including you. You are special. You are not just a student: you are a student athlete of your college or university. Represent your school well and with pride.

Think about your family when using social media, too. Because you are a student athlete, more eyes are on you and, of course, your family. Before you post anything, think about how what you are about to say might reflect on your loved ones. Does your post represent the values you were raised with? Stopping to consider your family could save your future.

Finally, think about yourself when you post to social media. Beyond what your post actually says, what does your act of sharing this specific post at this specific time say about you? How will that picture be interpreted? Does the post show that you are a good person? Does it suggest that you are the type of person we would like? Does it confirm that you are the kind of person we can trust? Does the post make you look like the type of person a hospital should invite to speak with sick children for a charity event? Is it the type of post that convinces a company like Nike that you would be a good spokesperson for them? You may say that social media is not who you are, but, in fact, it is absolutely a part of who you are, and a very public part, too. Whether you write it, picture it, or video record it, that post is an expression of you. So who do you want the world to see?

Remember that no one can record or document something you do not do. This is why you are the most important part of this whole social media thing. Everywhere you go, someone has a camera. Anyone with Internet access can see your social media posts. You are out there, people are watching, and you've got your brand to nurture. So carry yourself the way you want to be seen, say and post things that you would be proud to show your kids when they are your age, and remember that you control your image and message. Play social media like the athlete that you are: make every opportunity count, protect your team, and score big.

Stay Successful!
Jay Izso, the Internet Doctor®

NOTES

1. Dave Hawley, "Sex, Food and Selfies: Social Media's Dopamine Effect," *Adrants*, March 24, 2014, http://www.adrants.com/2014/03/sex-food-and-selfies-social-medias.php.
2. Kevin DeShazo, "Social Media Use of Student Athletes: 2016 Survey Results," *Fieldhouse Media*, April 13, 2016, http://www.fieldhousemedia.net/social-media-use-of-student-athletes-2016-survey-results/.
3. "Caitlin Ortiz, Molloy College Student, Loses Scholarship Because of Rap Lyrics on Her Facebook Wall," *Huffington Post*, June 20, 2011, http://www.huffingtonpost.com/2011/06/20/caitlin-ortiz-molloy-coll_n_880837.html.
4. "Cell Phone Use While Driving Statistics," *Edgar Snyder & Associates*, accessed July 27, 2016, https://www.edgarsnyder.com/car-accident/cause-of-accident/cell-phone/cell-phone-statistics.html.

ABOUT THE AUTHOR

JAY IZSO, the Internet Doctor ®, is a multi-award winning author, professional speaker, podcaster, and business/life coach. He works with entrepreneurs, professional associations, colleges and universities, and businesses of all sizes. Jay empowers his audiences to recognize the psychological needs of their clientele and imparts the tools and knowledge to build relationships and garner loyalty.

Having literally written the book on the subject, *Got Social Mediology? Using Psychology to Master Social Media for Your Business without Spending a Dime*, Jay Izso is a pioneer in the field.

Jay's upcoming three new titles to be released fall of 2018 include: *The Social Media Playbook for Student Athletes*; *The Social Media Playbook for Coaches & Administrators*; and *Lessons from the Farm: Essential Rules for Success*

Jay enjoys working with and motivating audiences all over the world. When he's not busy writing, speaking, and coaching, Jay enjoys life as a part-time beach freak, musician, sports fan, and classic movie buff. He lives in Raleigh, North Carolina, with his wife, Linda Craft, and their dog, Bandit.

Organizations and Memberships:
- National Speakers Association—Professional Member
- American Psychological Association

For more information about, his books,
or to book him for an event, visit:

www.jayizso.com

www.ingramcontent.com/pod-product-compliance
Lightning Source LLC
Chambersburg PA
CBHW031228050326
40689CB00009B/1516

*9 7 8 0 9 9 1 5 1 3 6 6 6 *